Tails and Tarradiddles

Such of these verses as appeared originally in *The Sydney Morning Herald* are reprinted here by courtesy of the proprietors.

*The Perfesser thinks it is a very good likeness of Alter Ego, Esq., and Alter Ego, Esq. thinks it is a very good likeness of the Perfesser, but neither of them thinks it is a good likeness of himself. People are like that about likenesses.*

# Tails and Tarradiddles

An Australian Book of Birds and Beasts

By THE PERFESSER and ALTER EGO,
Esquire

Tails and Tarradiddles: An Australian Poetry Book For Kids About Birds and Beasts.

© 2025

By Launcelot Harrison

Edited by Michelle Morrow

Images remastered by Sarah Graham

Paperback edition

ISBN: 978-1-7636291-6-5

Published by My Homeschool PTY LTD

NSW, Australia

This is a remastered version of the original book that was first published in 1925.

Original title: Tails and Tarradiddles: An Australian Book of Birds and Bees by The Perfesser and Alter Ego, Esquire.

This book is copyright. It is not for individual sale. Apart from any fair dealing for the purposes of private study, research, criticism or review as permitted under the Copyright Act, no part may be reproduced, stored in a retrieval system, or transmitted, in any form or by any means, electronic, mechanical, photocopying, recording or otherwise without prior permission.

All enquiries to My Homeschool PTY LTD
https://myhomeschool.com

TO 'PAT'

WHO SCORNS THE MORE DIGNIFIED TITLE

THAT IS HIS AND MINE

THESE INDISCRETIONS OF A GODFATHER

ARE MOST RESPECTFULLY DEDICATED

# EDITOR'S NOTE

I picked up this little gem 20 years ago while scouring a second hand bookshop. I'd never heard of it but I took a chance because it looked old and I loved the nature themes.

Wow! Was I pleased that I did. My children were delighted with it. They loved the author's quirky humour. It was a particular favourite with one of my sons when he was around 10.

Over the years I've shared it with others who also enjoyed it, but my antique book was falling apart. This year for its 100th anniversary I decided to put it back in print. We have included all the original illustrations and poems that were in the first edition.

This book was written by Launcelot Harrison, a distinguished Australian zoologist whose deep passion for the natural world began in his boyhood and later flourished into a celebrated academic career. Although known mostly for his academic writing, he published this children's poetry book under the pseudonym *The Perfesser and Alter Ego, Esquire*. This collection of whimsical, clever verse about Australian animals not only showcased his gift for illustration but also revealed his lighter, more imaginative side, delighting both children and adults alike.

In 1908, Launcelot married a celebrated Australian author, Amy Eleanor Mack. They lived in Sydney, NSW and together they shared a passion for nature and literature. They never had children. He dedicated this book to his godson, Pat.

Launcelot Harrison's life, though tragically cut short at 47 from a brain hemorrhage, was rich with scientific discovery, public service, and creative expression. His contributions, both scholarly and literary, continue to resonate, offering insights into Australia's diverse wildlife and the joys of storytelling.

Michelle Morrow

2025

# EXPLANATION

Some people prefer to wait for explanations until the end, but by then you have usually forgotten what they want to explain, so that is not of much use. It is much better to explain at the beginning, so that, when you come to anything, you know what the explanation is.

This book has two authors. One is the Perfesser, a really truly Perfesser, with carpet slippers and a long dressing gown, who is very wise. The other is Alter Ego, Esq., who is not so wise. The Perfesser is very polite. He always knocks at doors, and waits until he is asked to come in. He even knocks at the door of his own room, which is sometimes awkward; for, if there is no one inside to ask him in, he has to stay outside all night. It is because he is so polite that he has allowed Alter Ego, Esq., to write some of this book. All the very wise verses have been written by the Perfesser, and in these the natural history is perfectly correct. But if you come across any that are not wise, you will know that these have been written by Alter Ego, Esq., and he has forgotten all the natural history he ever knew. This would not matter so very much, only he will make it up out of his head. The pictures have also been done by Alter Ego, Esq., not because he can make pictures, but because the Perfesser was too polite to tell him not to.

The title of the book was made up by Alter Ego, Esq. The Perfesser wanted to call it 'Beneath the Eucalyptus,' but Alter Ego, Esq., said that was a silly name, because no one would know whether it meant Eucalyptus siderophloia or Eucalyptus corymbosa; while, if it were called 'Tails and Tarradiddles' everyone would know exactly what was meant.

# Table of Contents

EDITOR'S NOTE .................................................................... 9
EXPLANATION ..................................................................... 11
THE CRAKES ...................................................................... 17
PLATYPUS ........................................................................ 19
IN BED ........................................................................... 20
IN RUFFLES ...................................................................... 22
MRS KANGAROO .................................................................... 26
KING OF THE CASTLE .............................................................. 27
THE BUNYIP ...................................................................... 29
BLACK MAGPIES ................................................................... 31
MR. BANDICOOT ................................................................... 33
MISTER BUTCHERBIRD .............................................................. 34
BROLGAS ......................................................................... 35
THE WALLABY AND THE BULL-ANT ................................................... 42
SECRETS ......................................................................... 43
FLYING FOX ...................................................................... 45
TELLING TAILS ................................................................... 48
MISTER WAGTAIL .................................................................. 49
OLD MAN GOANNA .................................................................. 50
THE RABBIT AND THE EAGLEHAWK ................................................... 52
SILVEREYE ....................................................................... 55
 WALLAROO ....................................................................... 57
THE KOOKABURRA .................................................................. 59
THE RINGTAILS ................................................................... 60
THE LEATHERHEAD ................................................................. 63
THE SPINY ANTEATER .............................................................. 65
THE QUARRION AND THE BUDGERIGAR ................................................ 66
MY VEGEBUL GARDEN ............................................................... 70

| | |
|---|---|
| JACKY WINTER | 71 |
| MRS. KOALA | 73 |
| THE LITTLE SPARROW | 76 |
| POSSUM UP A GUM TREE | 78 |
| THE CURLEW THAT ISN'T THE CURLEW | 80 |
| MANNERS | 84 |
| HOW THEY WERE NAMED | 86 |
| THE MISTLETOE BIRD | 90 |
| THE OWL AND THE MOREPORK | 91 |
| THE TRIANTEWOBBEGONG | 94 |
| THE FANTAIL | 95 |
| THE WOMBAT | 96 |
| THAT TREE | 98 |
| FINIS | 99 |
| GLOSSARY | 101 |

## THE CRAKES

Do you know the Crakes that creep in the creek?
Or does nobody know them but me?
They're just like the great big Waterhens,
But tiny as tiny can be.

There's the Spotted Crake, and the Spotless Crake,
And the Little—Crake that's three;
But you've got to keep—Oo-ever so still,
If a Crake you want to see.

They creep in and out of the reeds and grass; They're as shy as ever can be;
You must lie quite still, and hold your breath,
If a Crake you want to see.

And then they will all come creeping out,
One—and two—and three;
They will point their toes and flick their tails,
As grown up as can be.

The Coot and the Redhill are great big birds,
And they're quite easy to see;
Still, the Crakes are grown up too, you know,
Although they are tiny-wee.

They are not black, and they are not blue,
But brown as ever can be;
And I suppose they're brown because
It makes them hard to see.

They're the loveliest darlings in all the creek,
Because they are so wee,
And because they creep, and sneak, and hide,
And because they're hard to see.

Don't you know the Crakes that creep in the creek?
O, why can't you ever see?
I sometimes think the fairies must
Have made them just for me.

## PLATYPUS

Platypus, Platypus, tell me as you float,
Why you have a duck's face with a furry coat;
Didn't you know really what you were going to be?
Now, don't look offended—you can surely tell me.

Platypus, Platypus, take me for a dive.
I only want to see how it is you keep alive.
What I want to know is, the dinner that you seek,
And how you ever catch it with your funny old beak.

Platypus, Platypus, show me where you hide
Your two furry babies in the creek-side;
Take me to their cradle, I shan't do them harm;
I only want to see you have them tucked up warm.

# IN BED

My bed's on the veranda, and, when I'm tucked up at night,
Mum always reads me stories underneath the 'lectric light;
And I like to hear the stories, but I simply love to look
At the little tiny creepy things that fly down on the book.

I don't mean creepy crawlies that Mum has to shoo away
Like the moths and buzzy beetles, that you never see by day.
But the little teeny weeny ones that run and skip and hop,
Not half so big as a comma—'bout the size of a full stop.

There's lots of different kinds of them, and they've proper legs and wings,

That glisten pearly in the light, and have heaps of veins and things;
And they've proper eyes, and some of them have feathers on their head;
And some don't have the feathers, but have whiskers there instead.

How they can pack them all about, I do not know at all;
You wouldn't think there'd be room enough, they are so very small;
And we have to blow them carefully, for fear the page should squeeze.
God must be awful clever to make tiny things like these.

## IN RUFFLES

Mother's lost her cameo,
A spoon's been lost by cook,
Dad can't find his silver stud—
Wherever shall we look?
Molly's lost her sapphire ring
And Peg her brooch of pearls;
Mother crossly says they are
A pair of careless girls.
All the homestead's quite upset
Because things can't be found,
And Father says that me and Tom
Had better look around.

Grown up folks are not so wise;
They're very ignorant.
That is why they never can
Find the things they want.
But me and Tom are only boys,
And many things we know

That grown ups never think about;
And one is where to go
When things are lost. We know at once—
We can find them any hour—
For all the things that are ever missed
Are down in Ruffles' bower.

Ruffles is our bowerbird,
At least we say he is;
He really isn't ours at all;
He's really only his.
He hangs about the kitchen door
Looking out for scraps;
And he and Mrs. Ruffles are
A jolly pair of chaps.
And up in the big Coolabah
They have a tiny nest;
But down by the tank they have their bower
And that's what we like best.

The bower's made of rows of sticks
That's stuck into the ground,
And every morning Ruffles comes
To play and play around.
He heaps between the rows of sticks
White sheep and rabbit bones,
And bits of glass, and shells of snails,
And brightly coloured stones;
And if he sees things lying round
That seem to suit his taste,
He whips in through the window and
He's off with them in haste.

But Ruffles isn't really bad,
He does it all for fun:
He likes all kinds of sparkly things
That glisten in the sun.
So when the folks are bothering
'Bout things that can't be found,
We just go off to Ruffles' bower
And take a look around.
And sure enough they're always there—
But of course we don't tell Dad,
Or Mum, or Moll, or Peg, or cook,
Because they'd just be mad.
But Bob, the groom, he knows a bit,
And fun he loves to poke,
And of me and Tom and Ruffles makes
A silly kind of joke.
For if we can't find Dobbin round
Or Strawberry, the cow,
He laughs a silly kind of laugh
And says to us well, now,
I saw that Ruffles round again
Today; if I were you
I'd have a look in Ruffles' bower,
Yes, that's what I would do.

But Bob's a silly sort of coot,
He don't mean to offend,
He doesn't realise, of course,
That Ruffles is our friend;
And we love to watch him playing games
And kicking up his legs,

While Mrs. Ruffles, up above,
Is sitting on her eggs.
Why do we call him Ruffles?
Well, that's surely plain enough—
Because he has around his neck
That lovely purple ruff.

## MRS KANGAROO

What have you in your bag today,
Mrs. Kangaroo?
Why, it's little Joey!
How do you do?

Whither are you taking him,
Mrs. Kangaroo?
'The silly little fellow
Wants to see the Zoo.'

Don't let them keep him there,
Mrs. Kangaroo;
If I lost my playmate,
What should I do?

# KING OF THE CASTLE

The Blue wren stood on a garden stick,
As proud as he could be;
And he tossed up his head, and he cocked up his tail,
And he said to himself, said he:

'I am the king of the castle,
And this is my castle fine;
It has twenty towers, and fifty rooms,
And sixty horses, and seventy grooms,
And a cellar full of wine.

'I am the king of the castle,
And this is my castle grand;
It has central heating, and hot-and-cold,
And a chest cram full of jewels and gold,
And an orchestra, and a band.

'I am the king of the castle,

And this is my castle tall;
There's a pergola covered with Morning Glory,
And a bush house, and a conservatory,
And grapevines on the wall—'

But a Little Tit, who was passing by,
Said 'Go on, you silly, that's all my eye
And Betty Martin, you booby; why,
Your castle's only a garden stick.
Your head may be blue, but it's blooming thick;
And as for your boasting, it makes me sick;
Go home and get tea for your wife and chick.'

And the Blue wren came to earth with a shock;
He was only a bird with his tail acock;
And the wonderful castle wasn't there;
He'd been building his castles in the air.

The Perfesser fear that the Little Tit
was not quite polite. In fact he asked
the Little Tit about it, and the little
Tit said—'You're quite right, Cocky,
my boy. Little Tits always are vulgar;
Little Tit always will be vulgar; Ting-
a-ling!'—and off he flew.

# THE BUNYIP

(Alter Ego, Esq., says this one is true, but the Perfesser does not know whether to believe him, or not.)

The Bunyip boomed in the billabong,
And the sheep they ran a mile,
And the lambs kicked up their heels and tails;
It made the Bunyip smile.

For the Bunyip loves a bit of fun,
And he hasn't an ounce of vice;
He is quite well bred, and is always fed

On porridge, and sago, and rice.

He likes to make a booming noise,
And frighten the folks about;
He loves to hear them whispering—
'Look out—the Bunyip's out.'

And what amuses him the most,
And fills his soul with glee,
Is to hear the silly story that
He's a seal come up from the sea.

But what annoys him dreadfully,
And clouds his face with gloom,
Is to hear men say that his lovely voice
Is only the Bittern's boom.

For the Bunyip does live in the billabong,
And is there for all to see;
Which is very well known to the sheep and lambs,
The Bittern, and you, and me.

## BLACK MAGPIES

Mad things—Mad things,
Here again with your black and white wings,
Here again with your black and white tails,
Here again with your mad, mad song—
    *Corowong, Corowong.*

Tell me, Maggies, why you're so mad;
Is it the winter that makes you glad?
What is it sends your chorus wild
Straight to the heart of a little child?

It isn't real music your voices make.
And I don't love you for your beauty's sake;
But there's something about you that makes me glad,

It must be because you are mad, you are mad.

*Ah-how-Ah-how-Corowong-Charrawack!*
Maggies, your voices take me back—
Back to the hills of a distant scene,
Back to the gullies that lay between;
Back, where you held me close in thrall
With the wild delight of your wild, wild call.
That rang up the range from the scrub below.
What is it, Maggies? I don't know.

Mad things—Mad things,
Hurrying, scurrying, tails and wings;
Racing, racing, through the trees.
Calling, calling, just as you please—
*Corowong, Corowong, Charrmack—*
Maggies, dear Maggies, take me back.
I can only be happy where you are—
Take me back to your hills afar.

Maggies, what is it that makes me glad?
It must be because you're so mad, so mad.

## MR. BANDICOOT

Snuffle and snort,
Snuffle and snort,
    Mr. Bandicoot!
Is it a worm you are after;
Is it a grub or a root?

Snuffle and snort,
Snuffle and snort,
    Mr. Bandicoot!
I don't like holes in my garden,
    Off—you—scoot!

## MISTER BUTCHERBIRD

Please,
Mr. Butcherbird,
What have you got
Today?
Can I have
Some roast beef?
What is that
You say?
Only got a caterpillar!
Not a mutton chop?
No,
Mr. Butcherbird,
I'll have to change
My shop!

## BROLGAS

Brolgas, Brolgas, out on the plain,
Do go on with your dance again—
    In and out, in and out,
    Set to partners and turn about
    Skip and hop, skip and hop,
    Flap your wings, and then you stop.

Brolgas, Brolgas, out on the plain
Dance for me, dance for me, once again;
Stretch your necks, and clap your beaks,
I could watch you for weeks

Brolgas, Brolgas, out on the plain,
Why do dance in the wind and rain?
>   In and out, in and out,
>   Set to partners and turn about
>   Skip and hop, skip and hop,
>   Flap your wings, and then you stop.

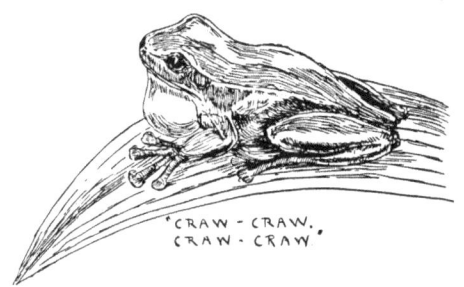

## THE FROGS

The old Green Frog in the bush-house is
    A terribly solemn thing;
He looks so old, and he looks so wise,
    You couldn't expect him to sing;
But there are times, in the summer days,
    When the rain goes 'Hiss-hiss-hiss,'
That he tunes up with his solemn croak,
    And it sounds a bit like this—
        'Craw-craw-Craw-craw.'

The Golden Frog, he lives in the pond,
    And he lives there in dozens,
With his brothers and sisters, his uncles and aunts,
    His nephews and nieces and cousins;
And they sing a chorus to make you deaf,
    Which you certainly wouldn't miss
If they didn't sing it for months again,
    And it goes a bit like this—
        'Craw-awk—crawk—crok-crok.'

"CREE-CREE-CREE—"

The little Grey Frog, he lives in the grass,
    And he is very jolly;
He sings his song the whole year round
    For he's never melancholy—
Winter and summer it's all the same,
    And I like that song of his;
He hurries so fast to get it out,
    And it sounds a bit like this—
        'Cree-cree-cree-cree-cree-cre,-cree.'

The little Brown Frog, he lives anywhere,
    In the gutter, or quarry, or creek,
And no one could possibly say about him
    That he isn't able to speak;
For he talks all the time, all the day, all the night,
    'S if he hadn't a moment to miss.
And he hasn't so much to talk about,
    For it only sounds like this
        'Crik-ik—Crik-ik—Crik-ik'

The Spotted Frog I don't often see,
    For he doesn't come to the top,
But he calls from under the water just
    As if he could never stop;
How he keeps the water from coming through
    Into that mouth of his
I cannot tell, but his funny song
    Just sounds a bit like this—
        'Cook-ook-ook-cook.'

"TOC"

The big Striped Frog hides amongst the rocks,
    And he hasn't got much to say—
Only one remark, which I often hear
    As about the creek I play;
It does get very monotonous,
    That single remark of his;
If I couldn't say more I should stay shut up,
    And it simply sounds like this—
        'Toc.'

"The Bull-ant sat on the Wallaby's tail."

# THE WALLABY AND THE BULL-ANT

The Wallaby sat on an ironbark stump,
     Budgeree, Budgeree, Bingy—
Wondering how far he was able to jump,
     Budgeree, Budgeree, Bingy.

The Bull-ant sat on the Wallaby's tail,
     Budgeree, Budgeree, Bingy—
And the Wallaby started off full sail,
     Budgeree, Budgeree, Bingy.

The Bull-ant's face wore a satisfied smile
     Budgeree, Budgeree, Bingy—
For the Wallaby found he could jump a mile,
     Budgeree, Budgeree, Bingy.

## SECRETS

Everyone knows the Jackass, and the Peewee, and the Thrush,
And lots of other birds that you can always see in the bush;
But I sometimes think I like the best (if you
know what I mean)
Those other birds, the little birds, the birds that are never seen.
You can often hear them squeakling in the thickets by the creek,
But you never can catch sight of them, however close you peek;
You can only hear a scratching sound in the places where they've been—

Those other birds, the little birds, the birds that are never seen.

I'm sure they're really birds, because I sometimes see a twig

Dancing where they have perched on it, so I know they can't be big;

But a dancing twig's the only sign that I can ever glean

Of those other birds, the little birds, the birds, that are never seen.

Sometimes I fancy that I see the flash of a bright eye,

Or just a glimpse of something brown and feathery passing by,

Though I can't be sure; but I like to feel that secrets lie between

Me and those birds, the little birds, the birds that are never seen.

## FLYING FOX

Flying fox, Flying fox, crossing the evening sky,

Tell me what you are seeking, up there so high, so high;

Not my peaches and nectarines, that would never do;

There are plenty of figs on the Moreton Bay quite good enough for you.

Flying fox, Flying fox, hanging above my head,

With your toes right up, and your nose right down, you look as though you were dead;

But you mustn't sleep in my wattle tree—that would never do;

There are plenty of trees in the bush outside quite good enough for you.

Flying fox, Flying fox, you are a funny chap,

Hung by the claws on your leathery feet, whenever you take a nap;

I have a bed in the nursery, but for you that wouldn't do;

Still, I'd love to sleep in the bush all night, in a tree alone with you.

"And the Diamond-bird's tail—if you call it a tail—
Is easy because it's so small."

# TELLING TAILS

The Lyre-bird's tail is easy to tell,
    For it's shaped just like a lyre,
And has two funny feathers stuck in it,
    Which are just like a piece of wire;
And the Black Cockatoo has an easy tail,
    For it's long and black and yellow,
And the yellow is striped with little black marks,
    And he is a great big fellow.

The Fantail's tail is easy, too,
    For it's like a feather fan,
And she opens it out and shuts it up
    As often as she can;
And the Bee-eater's tail you couldn't miss,
    No matter how hard you tried,
For its middle feathers stick right out
    From the little black feathers beside.

The Emu-wren's tail is so funnily made
    That it is quite simple to spot;
And I sometimes think this is just as well,
    For the rest of the bird is not;
And the Diamond-bird's tail—if you call it a tail—
    Is easy because it's so small
That if he didn't tell you you'd scarcely know
    That he had a tail at all.

# MISTER WAGTAIL

Fie, Mr. Wagtail, what is that you say?
*I'm a sweet pretty creature*—all the livelong day;
It does sound so conceited—really, don't you see,
You should leave the saying of things like that to me.

Fie, Mr. Wagtail, what is it you do—
Perched upon the cow's back, what has come to you?
Hopping round the cow's nose, snapping up the flies—
Fie, Mr. Wagtail, you fill me with surprise.

Fie, Mr. Wagtail, whatever are you at?
Why do you go chasing a poor Peewee like that?
What has Mr. Peewee done to you, I say?
Fie, Mr. Wagtail, you'd better fly away.

Fie, Mr. Wagtail, don't you be so bold;
I shall not be frightened, however much you scold;
I won't hurt your babies, you stupid sillikins;
I want to see their feathers coming through their skins.

Fie, Mr. Wagtail, what shocking hours you keep;
Whistling after bedtime, can't you go to sleep?
You'll wake all the babies, and give them such a fright,
With your sweet pretty creature all through the night.

# OLD MAN GOANNA

Old Man Goanna
Ran up a tree;
Old Man Goanna
Looked down at me.
Old Man Goanna,
Isn't he a fright?
His face would keep you
Awake all night.

Old Man Goanna
He stole an egg;
Then Towser got him
By his hind leg;
Cook caught him—Wallop!
And Bill caught him—Whop!
Old Man Goanna
Called out 'Stop!'

Old Man Goanna
Ran for his life;
So did his children
And so did his wife;
They all ran together,
And tumbled in the creek;
And we haven't seen them
Since last Tuesday week.

# THE RABBIT AND THE EAGLEHAWK

There was a Bunny Rabbit
And he lived beside a fence,
Which just went to show that
He had some common sense;
For there also was an Eaglehawk
Who lived up in a tree,
And he was very fond of
Bunny Rabbit for his tea.

The Eaglehawk flew down the fence,
Our Bunny he espied;
But when he swooped upon him,
Bunny skipped the other side.
He tried again, and yet again,
But every time he tried
He found that Bunny wasn't there
He'd skipped the other side.

The Eaglehawk perched on the fence
And sat awhile in thought,
Then said 'To you, my skittish friend,
A lesson must be taught.
You think you're very funny,
But I mean to have your life;
You wait a bit.' And off he went
Straight home to fetch his wife.

He said 'My dear, I much regret
Having to trouble you,
But ere we have our tea tonight
There's one thing we must do.
I need your aid in catching
This cheeky Bunny Rab,
Who dodges underneath the fence,
And so eludes my grab.

'Now I will fly upon this side,
And you will fly on that;
If I don't catch him my side,
You'll catch him yours, that's flat.
So leave the infants, darling,

And fly along the fence;
And this succulent young rabbit
Shall be your recompense.'

The Rabbit saw them coming,
And tumbled to their plan;
He tucked his tootsies under him
And for his hole he ran.
And as they swooped upon him,
One from either side,
He made a mighty effort
And just nipped down inside.

And as for the two Eaglehawks
Who thought to have his head
Instead of catching rabbits they
Just caught themselves instead.

## SILVEREYE

Lend me your glasses with silver rim,
     Silvereye, Silvereye;
I'd like to see—but my sight is dim—
     What you espy,
As you hop all over the wattle tree,
Prying, and picking, and pecking and poking,
I sometimes think you are only joking;
Can you find nothing at all for me—
Some of the sweets that the fairies make,
Or a taste of a dicky-bird's birthday cake?
With my poor eyes I can't see a thing;
Lend me your eye, with its silver ring.
Lend me a note of your sweet, sad song,
     Silvereye, Silvereye;
I'd like to sing it when things go wrong,

  And I want to cry.
Tears are the stupidest kind of things,
With sobbing, and sighing, and sopping, and seeping—
Boys and girls soon grow tired with weeping;
But you, little bird of the olive wings,
Salve your sadness with soft, sweet notes.
Song is better than sobs for throats.
So I ask you, when things go wrong,
Lend me a note of your sweet, sad song.

## WALLAROO

Wallaroo,
What'll we do?
I want to go fishing,
And so do you.

Wallaroo,
Here's what we'll do—
To the tip of your tail we'll tie the bait,
Then we will sit on the bank and wait;
When the fish bites, he will pull you,
You will pull him, and I'll pull you too;

Yes, Wallaroo,
That's what we'll do.

Wallaroo,
We shall have nice fish for our tea—
Cod for you, and perch for me;
Aren't you glad I came out with you?

# THE KOOKABURRA

On the signal arm;

Along there came
A train;

The

      arm

           went

                  down,

And

   so

      did

         Jack,

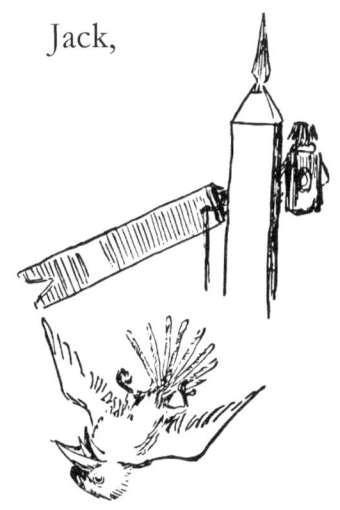

And he'll not

Sit there

Again

## THE RINGTAILS

Mister Ringtail built a nest
On a branch above the creek:
He didn't know much about architecture,
For he hadn't attended a single lecture,
But was full of theory and conjecture;
Nevertheless he did his best,
Nor knew that the branch was weak.

Mistress Ringtail came to watch
The building above the creek;
She herself was rather uneasy,
For the branch was thin, and the spot was breezy,
And the wind through the treetops whistled wheezy;
She thought the nest a bit of a botch,
But it wasn't her place to speak.

Mister Ringtail fussed about

With armfuls of twigs and leaves;
He didn't know much about building, but he
Determined to have it nice and jutty,
With heaps of bow-windows, all sticky and strutty,
And a nice front parlour peering out
Beneath overhanging eaves.

Said Mistress Ringtail—'Are you sure
It's safe? 'Twould be a blow
After all your work—I don't want to grumble
If the branch should break, or rot, or crumble,
And you and I and the children tumble—
Horrible thought I can't endure—
Right into the creek below.'

Mister Ringtail laughed with scorn,
And straightened his back with pride;
He said to his doubting wife 'My Blossom,
No truly domestic Ringtailed Possum
Who loved his children would wish to toss 'em
Into the water, all forlorn,
Along with his lovely bride.'

The family went to live in the nest,
But, lo and behold, one day
A tempest came with a terrible splutter,
And rain that ran right over the gutter,
And wind that set all the leaves aflutter;
All day long it stormed and stressed,
And it blew the nest away.

The little Ringtails fell through the tree,
And scraped from their tails the fur;
Each said as he went 'Well now, who'd have thought a
Ringtail would do what he didn't oughter,
And scrape his tail, and fall in the water;
I wonder what Ma will do to me
For so disobeying her!'

Mister Ringtail ran away
As fast as he possibly could;
He said as he ran 'Oh, woe betide me,
Whereabouts can I possibly hide me,
Before the Missus has really spied me?
Alas, what a very unfortunate day!'
And he hid himself in the wood.

The Ringtail family got to land,
A pitiful sight to see;
So cold and wet that they couldn't utter
A word—they could only stammer and stutter;
The sight of them made their mother mutter
'Great Gum Leaves, what a lovely band,
And to think they belong to me!'

# THE LEATHERHEAD

The Leatherhead sat in the cherry tree,
And the song that he sang was full of glee,
As he guzzled the cherries, three by three.

He bulged and he bulged till he truly just
Looked as though the next minute he'd surely bust;
The sight would make anyone sick with disgust.

And he sang as he gorged 'Oh, isn't it fine
Of the farmer to grow his trees line upon line,
So there's always another where I can dine.'

But the farmer's boy, after his work was done,
Strolled through the orchard, and carried his gun;
And he said 'I will spoil that old Leatherhead's fun.'

He lifted the gun, and he shut both his eyes,

And the trigger he pulled. What an awful surprise!
The old Leatherhead filled all the air with his cries.

He fluttered away with a rickety gait,
For the load in his tummy was far too much weight,
And he hadn't a rudder with which to keep straight.

For the shot that had pelted all round him like hail,
And had made him set up such a terrible wail,
Had blown every feather clean out of his tail.

He staggered off home, and he took to his bed,
With his featherless tail and his featherless head;
Now he doesn't eat cherries, but geebungs instead.

# THE SPINY ANTEATER

Stickly-prickly-Porky-pine,
What is it like on ants to dine?
Would you rather have your dinner than mine?

Stickly-prickly-spickety-spike,
I can eat whatever I like;
If they gave me ants, I should go on strike.

Stickly-prickly, how does it taste
To have your tongue all covered with paste
To stick the ants so they won't go to waste?

Stickly-prickly, upon my word,
You are really too absurd
To lay an egg like a dicky-bird.

Stickly-prickly-snivelly-snout,
You'd better mind what you're about;
Your baby's pins are all sticking out.

# THE QUARRION AND THE BUDGERIGAR

The Quarrion and the Budgerigar
Were quarrelling heart and soul;
For the Quarrion said the Budgerigar
Had stolen her nesting hole.

The Budgerigar said 'I had it first
And, anyway, it's a sorry 'un;
It's not good enough for a Budgerigar;
It's hardly fit for a Quarrion.'

The Quarrion screamed, getting red in the face,
'What horrible depravity!
How can you dare to say such things
Of a highclass nesting cavity!'

The Budgerigar yelled 'There's a hole in the roof,
And the draughts would freeze your marrow;
I wouldn't have the frowsy old place
If you brought it me on a barrow.'

The Quarrion cried 'Well, get out of it quick!'
But the other said 'May I burst
If I'll move myself for the likes of you,
When I tell you I found it first.'

Old Mrs. Galah came flying up
And said 'Time this was ended.
I'm looking for a house myself,
And this one will be splendid.'

She jumped inside and there she stayed
Before they could reprove her;
Then they learned from her screams she was stuck so tight
That nothing on earth would move her.

The Quarrion and the Budgerigar
Nearly burst their sides with laughter,
They forgot their quarrel and always were
The best of friends thereafter.

*"I want a vegebul garden
With a Paddymelon-tree."*

# MY VEGEBUL GARDEN

I want a vegebul garden
With a Paddymelon-tree;
I'd have lots of Paddymelons
To come and play with me.

I want a vegebul garden
With a bed for growing tripe;
To feed my Paddymelons on
After they are ripe.

I want a vegebul garden
To train an onion vine;
Tripe and onions would be nice
When we sit down to dine.

I want a vegebul garden
With a plum pudding plant;
So that we could always have
Plum pudding when we want.

Bob says I'm a silly—
Things don't grow on a tree;
But that can't stop you wanting them;
At least, it can't stop me.

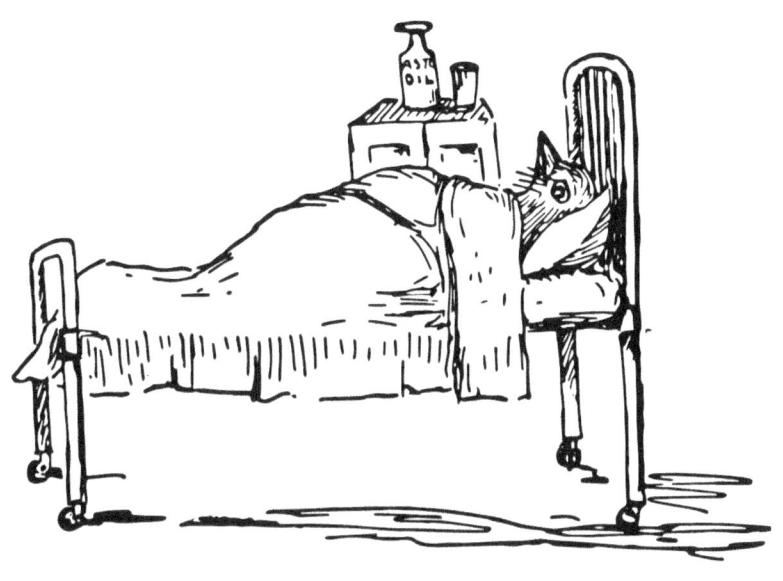

## JACKY WINTER

Jacky Winter got a splinter,
And it caused him pain;
Said his Ma 'I wot 'twill teach you not
To sit on posts again.

'I have told you oft that they are not soft,
But dangerous for your feet;
If to me you'll hark, you'll try strina-bark.
Whene'er you want a seat.'

The silly bird wouldn't heed her word,
But said 'Ma, I aspire
To higher things, while I have wings.'
So he sat on a telegraph wire.

At four o'clock an electric shock
Caught him a big surpriser;
No, he isn't dead—in a hospital bed
He's learning to be wiser.

## MRS. KOALA

Mrs. Koala really is
A very good Mamma,
For when she's got the breakfast, and
She's hustled off Papa,
She tidies all the children up—
And they are quite a bunch—
And gets them promptly off to school
With gum leaves for their lunch.

Then she does her housework, and
She tidies up the place;
Really, the mess that children make
Is a positive disgrace;
And she makes the baby's bottle warm,
But in this one thing she fails,
She never can remember when

To cut the baby's nails.

But that, perhaps, is just as well;
For, unlike you and me,
Mrs. Koala spends her life
Climbing about a tree;
For this she has to use her arms,
So of course can't carry her,
And baby has to go along
Clinging to Mamma's fur.

So when you see a baby bear
With claws as long as long,
I hope you will remember that
There's really nothing wrong;
And when *you've* carried baby till
Your arms are fit to crack,
P'raps you will wish that she had claws.
And could ride upon your back.

"While by his Waterbury watch
He counted minutes three."

# THE LITTLE SPARROW

There was a little Sparrow,
And he was out of work;
So he put his bluey on his back,
And he set out for Bourke.

He walked till he had bunions,
Then thought he would enquire;
But found that he had only got
As far as Nevertire.

He was hungry, and so weary
He could hardly drag a leg,
When suddenly, beside the track,
He found an Emu's egg.

He boiled it in his billycan,
And chuckled in his glee,
While by his Waterbury watch
He counted minutes three.

And when the minutes three were gone,
He thought it time to stop;
He took his little tomahawk
And he cut off the top.

'Twas a pity that he boiled it;
'Twould have been better fried,
For as he stooped to sup it up
He tumbled down inside.

And when he fell into the egg
He to his sorrow found
Three minutes wasn't long enough—
And the little chap was drowned.

The moral to this story is,
If Emu's eggs you seek
For supper, you should take great care
To boil them for a week.

## POSSUM UP A GUM TREE

Possum up a gum tree, look down at me;
Possum up a gum tree, what do you see?

For your babies, bread of my baking;
For your lady, gown of my making;
For yourself, a shoe and a sock;
I have them all in the lap of my frock.

Possum up a gum tree, come down to me;
A little girl is nicer than an old gum tree.

"And he turns his pockets inside out,
To show that the name is not hidden about."

# THE CURLEW THAT ISN'T THE CURLEW

The Curlew is a funny bird,
With legs so long that they're absurd,
And to make matters still more odd he
Has a head too big for his body.

The Curlew utters a mournful cry,
And has a large and sorrowful eye;
If you want the reason for this same,
It is because he has lost his name.

(The real Curlew is very superior,
He spends the winter in Siberia,
And has a long and beautiful beak,
Which reaches the middle of next week.

In autumn, when he sets off roamin',
He lends our Curlew his cognomen;'
But he wants it back the very first thing
When he comes down here for the spring.)

So our Curlew, it would appear,
Has a name for only half the year;
And there you have the cause, in brief,
Of the poor bird's heart-rending grief.

Kind friends have tried to fill the gap
By calling him 'Thick-knee, old chap;'
Which isn't in the best of taste,
And sends the Curlew off in haste.

Others have tried to smooth things over
By simply calling him 'Stone Plover;'
But this no consolation gives,
For there are no stones where the Curlew lives.

Still others call him 'Willaroo,'
Which makes the Curlew cry 'Boo-hoo,
What an awful name to give to me,
It sounds like a kind of Wallaby.'

What makes the Curlew weep and moan
Is that he once had a name of his own;
But he lost it many a year ago,
And this is the story, if you must know.

Long before there were me and you,
With a cargo of animals for the zoo
The good ship ark was sailing round,
When Captain Noah he ran aground.

He looked from the window, and said 'My hat,
We seem to have struck Mount Ararat,
And just at bedtime, too—what a bore!
We must get the animals all ashore.'

Then there was a frightful to-do,
As the animals tumbled out two by two;
And right in the midst of the flurry and rout
The electric light went completely out.

The mate went to see, and he cried 'Yo-ho,
The Walrus is caught in the dynamo;'

And he tried to put the matter right
By blowing him out with dynamite.

But he failed, and they had to disembark
As best they could in the inky dark;
There were lots of things that they couldn't find.
And all these had to be left behind.

The Elephant, though he thunk and thunk,
Had quite forgot where he put his trunk;
The Fox lost his brush, and the Cock his comb,
And without these both refused to go home.

But it was much better when morning came,
For they found them all but the Curlew's name;
And though they turned everything inside out
They couldn't find this anywhere about.

Captain Noah said 'Now, don't make a fuss,
You just leave everything to us;
When we've finished unloading, I'll be bound
That your name most certainly will be found.

'So there is no need to squeal and bellow,
You toddle along like a good young fellow;
But before you go, leave me your address,
And I'll send your name by the Parcel Express.'

So every year, out at Dingo Flat,
When the parcels van comes from Ararat,
The Curlew asks Abdul Aboo the same
Old question—'Well, have you brought my name?'

And Abdul shakes his swarthy head,
For Captain Noah is long since dead;
And he turns his pockets inside out,
To show that the name is not hidden about.

So, in the dusk, when you'll be hearing
The Curlew wailing round the clearing,
You'll know that he is hoping still
For his name to be found—but it never will.

## MANNERS

The Kookaburra sits all fluffled up, you'd think he'd never been taught;
He gets round shouldered and stoopy through not sitting as he ought;
And he laughs too loud, and he laughs too long, and he's not polite like me;
I expect it's because he just lives in a hole, instead of a house, you see.
The Grey Thrush sits up nicely—he was reared in a proper nest,
And his voice is sweet, and he's never cross, and I like him one of the best;
But the Little Tits are awful; they just won't keep still a bit,
And they keep on fidgeting all the time, with their 'Chit-chit-chit-chit-chit."

The Peewee is a stately bird, as he walks about the grass,
And he points his toes out just like us, when we go to Dancing class;
But the Spinebill's very restless, for he never can keep still, As he hurries and scurries from flower to flower with his long and slender bill.
But the Yellowbob's a darling, with grey back and yellow breast;
He has the nicest manners, and he makes the nicest nest;
And I like him best at picnics, when he sits on the side of a tree;
He wouldn't ask, but you know he means 'Isn't there a crumb for me?'

# HOW THEY WERE NAMED

Captain Cook, he came ashore,
With Banks and Dr. Solander;
They tied their boat to the monument,
And set off through the bush to wander
And the shrubs and the trees were all so strange,
And the flowers so bright and gay,
That Banks said to Cook 'I think you will have
To call this place Botany Bay.'

A little bird sat on the top of a bush,
And his wings were black and yellow;
His eye was bright, and his eye was white,
And he was a saucy fellow;

And he said 'What you find in those stupid shrubs
I really cannot see;
When there's beautiful birds like me about,
Why not name it after me?'

They took no notice, but wandered on,
And they hadn't wandered far,
When Dr. Solander stopped in front
Of a beautiful Waratah;
And he called out excitedly 'Banks, my boy,
Here's the loveliest kind of plant;
I have never seen quite the like before,
I must call it after my aunt.'

Arid Banks came running, and straightway said,
'Yes, I would if I were you;
Your Aunt Telopea's a perfect dear,
That's just the thing to do.'
But the rude little bird from the top of the bush
Yelled out 'I don't agree;
When there's birds as lovely as me about,
You should name it after me.'

Then Banks and Solander grew annoyed,
And even Cook was stirred;
They swore they would all be stricken deaf
By this pertinacious bird;
And Solander said 'He talks Double Dutch;'
And Banks said 'He eats honey,
So we'll call him the New Holland Honeyeater,
Just for being funny.

'And we'll call the country New Holland, so
That he'll think we've given in;
And perhaps he'll be satisfied with that,
And spare us his noisy din;
But we'll alter it quickly upon the maps,
As soon as the good ship sails;

So that he'll never know, after we have gone,
That it's really New South Wales.'

So the New Holland Honeyeater sits on a bush,
Though you go wherever you choose—
To Botany, Collaroy, Bondi, Dee Why,
Coogee or La Perouse—
And he screams and he shouts—for he still believes—
'The country as far as you see
Is my country, and I am the king of it all,
For they named it after me.'

The Perfesser says there is something wrong about this. They couldn't have tied their boat to the monument, because it wasn't put there till afterwards; and Dr. Solander did not have an Aunt Telopea—at least, he couldn't find her in the Public Library; and the country was called New Holland before Cook came there.
But Alter Ego, Esq., says it is all right, because he has a Poet's Licence.

# THE MISTLETOE BIRD

Of all the birds about the bush
The busiest I know
Is the Mistletoe bird, because he has
To plant the mistletoe.

His back is blue, and his breast is red:
He's a fusspot, too, I know;
But then, you see, he has to be,
To plant the mistletoe.

If he didn't do it there's nobody would,
And the mistletoe couldn't grow;
And the trees wouldn't look so pretty without
Their beautiful mistletoe.

He eats the berries, and keeps the seed,
And puts it on branches to grow;
And it's very hard work for a little bird
To be planting mistletoe.

He flies so far, and he flies so high,
And he whistles to me below
As he hurries across the land so wide
To plant his mistletoe.

He has planted all over Australia now,
As far as he can go;
But he hasn't had time for Tasmania yet,
So it has no mistletoe.

# THE OWL AND THE MOREPORK

The Boobook Owl was angry
As he sat up in the gloom,
While the old Morepork called softly
*'Oom-Oom-Oom.'*

The Boobook Owl said 'Morepork!
Hark to his stupid boom!
He can't say Morepork, or anything else
But *Oom-Oom-Oom.*

'These empty-headed humans
Will drive me to my tomb;
Imagine mixing me with him
And his *Oom-Oom-Oom!*

'It comes of his sitting about by day
Instead of keeping his room,

When I say *Morepork*, they think it is him!
Old *Oom-Oom-Oom.*'

The Morepork didn't answer back,
For this is the Morepork's doom—
He can't say anything else besides
'*Oom-Oom-Oom.*'

"He's a face like a face in the dark."

Tails and Tarradiddles

# THE TRIANTEWOBBEGONG

(The Perfesser says not to be frightened. This is one of
Alter Ego Esq.'s imaginary animals.)

Do you know that terrible creature,
The Triantewobbegong?
I wouldn't like him to meet you;
Let's hope he won't come along.

The front of him's like a spider,
The back of him's like a shark;
He's covered on top with a carpet,
He's a face like a face in the dark.

In front he has legs by the dozen,
Behind he has fins by the score;
His tail goes as far as you can see,
And beyond that a mile or more.

You sometimes find him in corners,
Or creeping about a wall;
But he's happier far in bumborahs,
That rise in an easterly squall.

Goodness knows what he feeds on—
I've never waited to see;
But that doesn't matter so long as
He doesn't catch you, or me.

# THE FANTAIL

    Ftit-a-
    Flirt-a-
    Fantail—
Flutter down the creek;
    Once his tail
    Is open,
Can't shut it for a week;
    All he has
    To sing about,
Just a little squeak;
    All he has
    For supper, just
A 'squito in his beak;
    Flit-a-
    Flirt-a-
    Fantail—
Flutter down the creek.

# THE WOMBAT

The Wombat isn't beautiful,
And hasn't any grace,
And his toes turn in when they should turn out;
But he has an honest face.

The Wombat doesn't talk much,
But not because he can't;
He was told that he mustn't, when he was young,
By his elderly maiden aunt.

The Wombat doesn't eat much,
You'll notice as you pass;
For all that he wants for his supper at night
Is a ton or two of grass.

The Wombat doesn't work much,
He only digs a hole;
But it is so wide, from side to side,
You'd think he was digging for coal.

The Wombat isn't useful,
Except for a kind of lark,
For the only use that he really has
Is to fall over in the dark.

The Wombat isn't beautiful,
And hasn't any grace;
But I love him dearly just the same
He's such an honest face.

# THAT TREE

'Twas the Tomtits that began it,
For they told the birds, you see,
That they always liked to make their nest
In a Monkey Puzzle Tree.

But the Thickhead, down from Queensland;
Said, while at King Billy's gunyah,
The King himself had told him that
The tree was a Bunya-bunya.

While the Peewee from the Gardens,
Just to make himself contrarier,
Said he'd often read the label and
It was Bidwill's Araucaria.

So then they fell to quarrelling
Till all were sore and sickly;
And decided that, whatever its name,
The tree was far too prickly.

"*A most lovely picture of that handsome bird the Pelican.*"

# FINIS

Said Alter Ego to the Prof. 'Oh, I know very well I can
Make a most lovely picture of that handsome bird the Pelican,
If you would only write the verse, and didn't simply shirk it all,
And leave the burden all to me, and really do no work at all.'

Said the Perfesser, 'You young scamp, you don't know what I'm suffering,
As I contemplate the consequences of your awful

duffering;
Of my scientific reputation you've not left a particle,
I shall never have the courage to indite another article.

'But the most disastrous feature of your glib and facile diction is,
You've dithered me so that I cannot tell what fact or fiction is;
Instead of doing your fair share both truthfully and rightfully,
You have deceived the birds and beasts and all the children frightfully.

'It's ages after bedtime, and I very much prefer to go
To bed myself before your silly rubbish gives me vertigo.
Now, no more words! to bed you go, for, though the book is thinnish, it
Is high old time to sit on you, and write 'The End,' and finish it.'

# GLOSSARY

Since the popular names used in this book are not universal, the scientific names of the animals and plants are given below. The bird names are those given in Leach, *An Australian Bird Book*, 2nd Edition, Melbourne, 1912; those of the beasts are as in Lucas and Le Souef, *The Animals of Australia*, Melbourne, 1909.

## BIRDS

| | |
|---|---|
| Bee eater | *Merops ornatus* |
| Bittern | *Botaurus poeciloptilus* |
| Black Cockatoo | *Calyptorhynchus funereus* |
| Black Magpie | *Strepera graculine* |
| Blue wren | *Malurus cyanochlamys* |
| Boobook Owl | *Ninox boobook* |
| Bowerbird | *Chlamydera maculata* |
| Brolga | *Antigone australasiana* |
| Budgerigar | *Melopsittacus undulatus* |
| Butcherbird | *Cracticus destructor* |
| Coot | *Fulica australis* |
| Crake, Spotted | *Porzana fluminea* |
| Spotless | *Porzana plumbea* |
| Little | *Porzana palustris* |
| Curlew (True) | *Numenius cyanopus* |
| (Stone Plover) | *Burhinus grallarius* |
| Diamond-bird | *Pardalotus punctatus* |
| Eaglehawk | *Uroaëtus audax* |
| Emu | *Dromaius novae-hollondiae* |
| Emu-wren | *Stipituru malachurus* |
| Fantail | *Rhipidura albiscapa* |
| Galah | *Cacatua roseicapilla* |
| Jacky Winter | *Microeca fascinans* |
| Jackass, or Kookaburra | *Dacelo gigas* |

# BIRDS

| | |
|---|---|
| Leatherhead | *Tropidorhynchus corniculatus* |
| Little Tit | *Acanthiza nana* |
| Lyrebird | *Menura superba* |
| Mistletoe bird | *Dicaeum hirundinaceum* |
| Morepork | *Podargus strigoides* |
| New Holland Honeyeater | *Meliornis novae-hollandiae* |
| Peewee | *Grallina picata* |
| Pelican | *Pelecanus conspicillatus* |
| Quarrion | *Calopsittacus novae-hollandiae* |
| Redbill | *Porphyrio* |
| Silvereye | *Zosterops coerulescens* |
| Sparrow | *Passer domesticus* |
| Spinebill | *Acanthorhynchus tenuirostris* |
| Thickhead | *Pachycephala rufiventris* |
| Thrush | *Colluricincla harmonica* |
| Tomtit | *Acanthiza chrysorrhoa* |
| Wagtail | *Rhipidura tricolor* |
| Yellowbob | *Eopsaltria australis* |

# BEASTS

| | |
|---|---|
| Bandicoot | *Perameles nasuta* |
| Bull-ant | *Myrmecia tarsata* |
| Flying fox | *Pteropus poliocephalus* |
| Frog, Brown | *Crinia signifera* |
| Frog, Green | *Hyla coerulea* |
| Frog, Golden | *Hyla aurea* |
| Frog, Gray | *Hyla ewingi* |
| Frog, Spotted | *Limnodynastes tasmamensis* |
| Frog, Stripped | *Limnodynastes peroni* |
| Frog, Goanna | *Varanus varius* |
| Kangaroo | *Macropus giganteus* |
| Koala | *Phascolarctus cinereus* |
| Paddymelon | *Macropus thetidis* |
| Platypus | *Ornithorhynchus anatinus* |
| Possum | *Trichosurus vulpecula* |
| Rabbit | *Lepus cuniculus* |
| Ringtail | *Pseudochirus peregrinus* |
| Spiny Anteater | *Echidna aculeata* |
| Wallaby | *Macropus ualabatus* |
| Wallaroo | *Macropus robustus* |
| Wombat | *Phascolomys mitchelli* |

# PLANTS

| | |
|---|---|
| Bunya Bunya | *Araucaria Bidwillii* |
| Coolabah | *Eucalyptus microtheca* |
| Geebung | *Persoonia spp.* |
| Gum | *Eucalyptus spp.* |
| Mistletoe | *Loranthus spp.* |
| Moreton Bay (Fig) | *Ficus macrophylla* |
| Stringy-bark | *Eucalybtus obliqua* |
| Waratah | *Telopea speciosissima* |
| Wattle | *Acacia spp. esp. Baileyana* |

www.ingramcontent.com/pod-product-compliance
Lightning Source LLC
Chambersburg PA
CBHW052149070526
44585CB00017B/2042